I0191408

Character Matters

Book 1

Michelle Sussman

/ BookLeaf
Publishing

India | USA | UK

Made with ❤ on the BookLeaf Publishing Platform
www.bookleafpub.in
www.bookleafpub.com

Dedication

For my father,
Philip Arthur Sussman (1951-2025)

Preface

Acknowledgements

1. Rose

Rose waits in her garden
For her love to come along.
She opens her arms wide
And sings in the rain.
Opening her petals to the sun,
She waits for the rays to beat down on her.
At the entrance of nightfall,
She closes her petals
And gets ready to sleep.
An innocent flower
Playful as can be,
Longing to jump rope and play hopscotch.
She waits in the sunshine
And stares up at the clouds.
A lonely rose in a huge garden
Waiting for her friends,
Impatient like a young child
Waiting for a present.
She longs to be sprinkled with love,
That poor lonely Rose.

2. June

There once was a woman named June.
She went to the store to buy spoons.
She found, by surprise —
A pair of green eyes!
Thus she brought home a Maine Coon.

3. Pam

There once was a woman named Pam.
She appeared as docile as a lamb.
Yet she had a short fuse.
Upon hearing bad news,
Her door would swing shut with a slam.

4. Multicolored Plants

Multicolored plants:
Delightful in gradients;
Layers of beauty.

5. Wildflowers of Texas

Las flores de Tejas—Hello, lovely ones!
As they dance in the breeze, they lift their petals to the sun.
They tilt their heads, listening
To English and Spanish swirling around them.
They watch the birds pecking at their seeds,
Cows and horses grazing.
They flit as cats, dogs, and people sniff them.
For as little as they care about politics,
The wildflowers of Texas
Detest the GOP for what they have become,
All the lies and corrupt
As they capitulate to Trump.
The wildflowers of Texas
Are great judges of character.
So what gives them hope?
How do they stay resilient?
Strong roots,
Compassion,
Clean air and water,
Tranquility,
Humility,
And gratitude.

6. Walter

There once was a man named Walter.
In speech, he tended to falter.
Then he found a girlfriend;
Thus, on the weekend,
He broke free of his fear—and he called her.

7. Transition to Autumn

Soaking up the last dose of warm weather,
The birds cruise the sky
And glide around the clouds.
They get tempted by the cumulus clouds,
So soft, white, and fluffy;
Oh, for a weary bird to rest in a cloud.
But it cannot—at least it has the trees
For nesting, and for respite.
Everybody loves the trees. Why?
Trees are beautiful, of course.
In spring and summer, they produce green leaves, and
Fruit, flowers, acorns and pine cones,
Depending on the species.
They create a natural frame for photos.
They yield shade and oxygen,
Home to birds and other wildlife,
And a place for kids to play.
In the transition to autumn, one may find
A mix of color—red, orange, yellow, brown, and green—
On neighboring trees,
Even on a single tree.
Squirrels and birds make their rounds
In the trees and on the ground,
As they greet me on my early-morning walks,

And my afternoon trips to the coffee shops.
Cicadas have their moment,
Hidden from view yet making their presence known,
Delighting me with their whirring.
Fireflies emerge at night with their enchanting glow.
Look at them, cherishing this slice of time
Known as the transition to autumn.

8. Happy Birthday, Jane!

Tourists from all over the world
Congregate in Bath, England,
Dressed in Regency clothes.
What is the occasion
That draws such an auspicious crowd?
Two and a half centuries ago,
A baby girl was born,
And as the years went by,
She would hone her writing skills—
First for the entertainment of her own family,
Then to share with the rest of the world.
Though she lived a short life,
Jane Austen published six novels,
Through which she is immortalized
With an impactful legacy.
Colin Firth as Mr. Darcy,
Blake Ritson shifting from hero to villain.
Elinor and Marianne—sisters who are as different
As night and day.
Anne Elliott second-guesses her breakup with Captain
Wentworth—
A breakup prompted by persuasion from a neighbor.
In a world of Mary Crawfords,
Be a Fanny Price.

Happy birthday, Jane!
As a wise man once said:
You're only 250 once,
But you're great 365 or 366 times a year.

9. Squirrels at the Window

Squirrels at the window,
Clamoring for attention
And delicious treats.

10. Bridget O'Rourke

A long time ago, in upstate New York,
There lived a kind woman named Bridget O'Rourke.
Her marvelous violin skills, adventurous spirit, intellect
and fluty laugh
Delighted everyone around her,
Especially her husband, Martin—a World War I veteran.
Behind Bridget's carefree demeanor
Lies a painful secret
Known only to family and a few close friends.
She lost her parents to influenza
When she was only seven.
She was sent to the orphanage,
Where she suffered mistreatment.
One fateful day, Bridget was rescued
By a dear friend, a soon-to-be sister
Who would dote on her for years to come;
Adopted by a childless couple
Whose love was as strong as hers and Martin's.
In her new family, Bridget now had:
A father who made dad jokes before it was cool;
A mother who advocated for women's right to vote;
And a sister who dreamed of opening a school.
Soon the household grew to include
Two more girls and a boy.

When meeting Martin at age fifteen, she fell in love.
She worried about him throughout his deployment—
Her heart heavy, yet she remained strong for him.
More often than not, she found herself
Crying in her sleep over nightmares
Of Martin dying in battle.
This triggered bad memories
Of her parent's deaths,
As she cried every night at the orphanage.
When the war was over and Martin came home,
The two of them wept and embraced,
Reluctant to let go.
When he proposed, she sang, "Yes."
In 1919, they were married in a church in New York City,
With a honeymoon in the Adirondacks.
For the next 48 years, Martin and Bridget
Lived in upstate New York,
As the proud parents of five, grandparents of eighteen,
And beloved aunt and uncle of many.
In 1969, on the day that would have been their fiftieth
wedding anniversary,
Martin laid a bouquet of roses and a tear-stained love
letter at Bridget's grave.
Family stories change, but love always remains.

11. Shy Little Sigrid

With her chocolate-brown hair and crystal-blue eye,
Shy little Sigrid slips in the classroom,
Making a beeline for her desk.
With the exceptions of greetings and "Thank you,"
She keeps to herself most of the day.
Eyes on the blackboard, eyes on the teacher,
But not a word passes her lips.
She completes all her homework.
She does well on her tests.
Yet she won't ask for help
Or to join games at recess.
Sigrid is like a crocus
Peeking out from the shelter of its own petals,
Waiting for the arrival of spring.

12. Emily and Taylor

A fictitious meeting between Emily Dickinson and Taylor Swift

"Taylor, my dear cousin," said Emily,
As they hugged each other in the hallway.
These two ladies from different centuries
Have taken the time to visit today.
They have different styles to their shared talents—
Taylor is fearless in sharing her words,
Whereas Emily is reticent
About her poetry publicly heard.
They met in the parlor—their special place
For tea and chatting about anything.
A gleeful smile lit up Taylor's face
As sunlight reflected onto her ring.
Then Emily knew she'd soon tie the knot;
She wished Taylor well, right there on the spot.

13. Character Matters

Social media—a double-edged sword:
When used for good, it nurtures connections;
Uplifting voices of those most adored,
Supporting them in their prized professions.
When used for evil, it loses its charm.
Cyberbullying and dishonest news.
Do not be "that person " inflicting harm
By feigning disabilities for views.
Respect is one thing money never buys;
What goes online can stay up forever.
When influencers lure you in with lies,
Their worlds collapse with each tie they sever.
Character matters—fame fades before long.
Free speech is a right, but don't use it wrong.

14. Antazil, Bondur, and Yoko

In honor of John Lennon and Yoko Ono

Alberto Chimal shares a powerful lesson for us all.
In his story, *El juego mas antiguo* (The Oldest Game),
Starring Antazil and Bondur—two witches, sworn
enemies.
For one witch's misfortune, the other was to blame!
Their respective supporters swore to never mention the
name
Of the other witch—this feud was no game.
One day, Antazil and Bondur agreed to a duel.
What was their aim?
To subdue her enemy, and put her to shame.
Throughout the duel, which was hardly tame,
Each witch transformed herself, in order to claim
Dominance over one another, refusing to take the blame,
Until they learned the truth:
They were one and the same!
Stop shunning Yoko—she doesn't deserve hate.
Cease your accusations before it's too late.
Be considerate of others and what they're going through.
Don't wait for the same thing to happen to you.

15. Ode to Nannerl Mozart

Maria Anna Mozart—affectionately known as Nannerl,
A talented musician living in her little brother's shadow;
Unable to flourish in the world of music as a woman,
Despite Wolfgang's encouragement for her to follow her
dreams.
Had Leopold Mozart granted both of his children
Equal opportunities to prosper,
Nannerl would have enriched the world of classical
music,
Alongside Wolfgang, and on her own,
With scores of gems;
Her creative juice flowing from her quill,
Like water flowing from a well.
Yes, Nannerl had accomplished various things
That most girls in the eighteenth century
Could neither fathom nor attain:
Traveling around Europe; showcasing her musical
prowess for royal families;
Celebrating her birthday in six countries.
(I'm a little jealous.)
Yet at age eighteen, she lamented the injustice of
inequality.
Resigned to her father's expectations,
She parted with her dreams,

Filling the void inside her

By working in Salzburg as a piano teacher.

Between music lessons, keeping house, and raising
children,

Nannerl accepted her lot, yet she envied her brother

For all the opportunities that she had been denied.

A change of heart on Leopold's part

Would have allowed Nannerl's output to grow.

Her hopes and dreams unearthed from a treasure chest,

Like America as it would have been,

Had Kamala Harris won the 2024 election.

16. The Oak Tree

The oak tree stands tall,
Reaching out to birds and squirrels.
Giving shelter to all who need it.
Calm against chaos.

17. Geri and Violet

Geri and Violet—college roommates and best friends,
both from Iowa.
When you see them together, you could say,
They're like Anne and Diana
Reimagined for modern day.
To think, when they first met,
That they wouldn't get along.
Violet, with her long raven-black hair and dark-blue
eyes,
Has been at loose ends with her friends—
Until she met Geri.
Auburn-haired Geri does it all!
When the girls first met,
Geri took offense
To the icy reception from Violet;
As Geri later learned,
Violet had been in the throes of depression.
As a Bronte fan, Violet attempted
To find solace in *The Tennant of Wildfell Hall.*
Big mistake!
That book exacerbated her depression!
"I wish I'd never read *The Tennant of Wildfell Hall!*"
She thought on move-in day.
Within a few weeks of the semester,

Violet had slowly but surely
Opened up to Geri
About her anxiety and depression.
For the first time in her life,
Violet had confidence
In a lasting friendship.

18. Ode to KidSpeak

Boys and girls from around the world
Step up to share their native languages
With friends who are eager to broaden their minds.
This wonderful group of children
Star in a computer program called KidSpeak:
A program packed with games, songs, and fun
animations;
Modules for the alphabet, numbers, and more.
What could be more fun
Than learning a new language
While playing games with a friend?

19. Raini

Rhiannon Leslie Winthrop is a typical London girl.
Always playing and dancing in the sun and rain--hence her nickname, Raini.
Intuitive by nature, she is.
Now 26, she has become a nurse.
In her home, she has a large collection of books and a garden.

20. Summer 2019

When I was growing up, a typical summer for me
Consisted of the following activities:
Reading, writing, drawing, movies, picnics and photo
trips;
Visiting relatives in Connecticut and New York;
Trips to the library, bookstores, and mall.
In Pittsburgh, I watered the garden in the backyard.
I loved listening to music on car rides.
I looked forward to back-to-school shopping—
The thrill of having new notebooks, folders, pencils, and
uniforms—
Despite pining for an extended summer.
Having a summer birthday
Has always been a blessing.
Looking back on the summer of 2019,
I must say, it was the best summer I've ever had
Since my graduation from Ohio University.
Every day had a feel, unlike summers in retail.
Early-morning walks on the bike path were the norm.
In the summer of 2019, I discovered on the bike path
Barn swallows swooping through the sky,
Building nests along the underside of a bridge.
A male cardinal surprised me
With a five-note call I'd never heard before.

A heron picked a fight with an unsuspecting egret
Over the best spot to catch fish in the river.
I kept a gratifying routine
In the summer of 2019:
Outings in nature in the morning,
Afternoons at libraries and coffee shops,
And movies or TV after dinner.
Once a week: Spanish Conversation Hour,
With dinner at an authentic Mexican restaurant.
Once a month: Silent Book Club,
In which readers bring their own books,
Share them with the group,
And silently read them onsite for an hour.
"Sustained Silent Reading,"
In the words of Ramona Quimby.
Phil's Fast and Friendly Pickup and Dropoff Service
Was in full swing in summer 2019.
It wasn't perfect, yet this chapter of my life
Was simultaneously reminiscent
Of summer vacations before 2016,
And a vista of my future.

21. Sir Kennedy

Enter Sir Kennedy:
An Englishman of impeccable taste,
A brilliant mind, a gregarious mien,
And a strong moral compass.
Ask him anything about the classics,
Be it classical music or literature,
And he'll give you a thoughtful answer.
If he doesn't know the answer, he admits it;
Owning up to his mistakes, he had learned the hard way.
In his youth, he prided himself
On being the smartest boy in the class.
Always the first to raise his hand
To answer the teacher's questions:
Grinning at every correct answer,
Or groaning under his breath
At every wrong answer given by his peers.
While Sir Kennedy excelled in academics,
His schoolmates (even his close friends)
Harbored resentment of his arrogance.
Believing he was destined for a career in academia or
politics,
He fancied himself a modern-day Romantic poet,
Or a British foil to John F. Kennedy.
As time went by, he ate humble pie;

He began helping others only for their sake, not his own.
Nothing could be finer to Sir Kennedy
Than making a difference in the world,
No matter how small.
Now his peers look upon him
As a venerable man, worthy of knighthood.
As a result, Sir Kennedy
Relishes their admiration for his humanity,
As well as his intelligence.

www.ingramcontent.com/pod-product-compliance
Lightning Source LLC
Chambersburg PA
CBHW051000030426
42339CB00007B/412